Upnor Castle

Jonathan Coad

CONTENTS

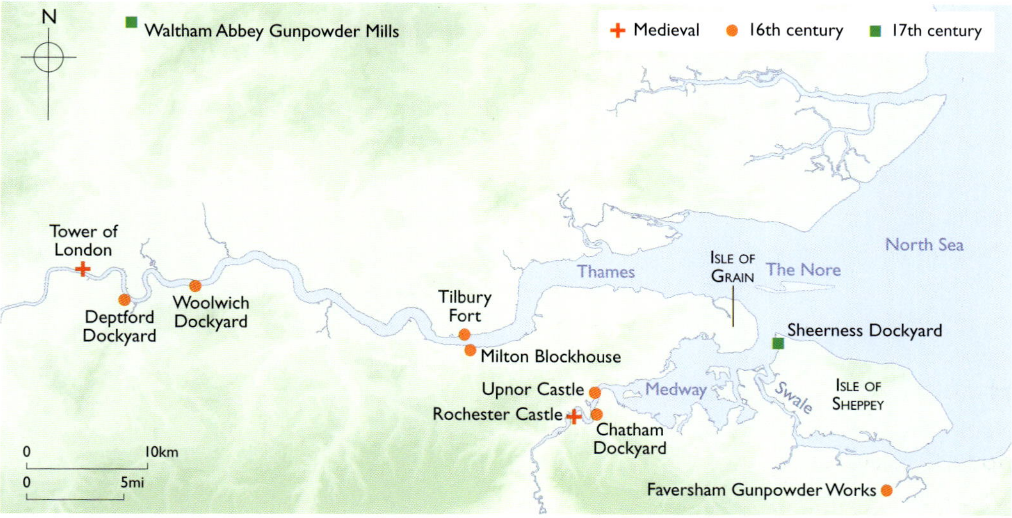

Tour of Upnor Castle

OVERVIEW AND SETTING

When Upnor Castle was built, between 1559 and 1567, the lower Medway area was largely rural, an agricultural landscape of scattered farms and small communities, many of which had developed beside the river or its creeks. The inhabitants worked as shipbuilders or fishermen, or manned the small sailing vessels trading with London or coastal towns.

The arrival of the Royal Navy in the early 16th century gradually altered this landscape, eventually transforming the small villages of Chatham and Gillingham adjacent to the fleet anchorage into sprawling conurbations. In the 1540s the obsolete Queenborough Castle, which had been built in the 1360s, was modified for artillery and garrisoned, and three small gun batteries, or blockhouses, were built: two 'within the isles of Sheppey and Grain' (originally named after their agricultural use) and one at Sheerness.

In 1550 the Medway was formally adopted for the mooring of the Navy's warships, requiring more substantial defences. In 1559 six 'indifferent [impartial] persons' chose a site for Upnor Castle on the wooded north bank of the river, from where its guns could protect the fleet from raiders and prevent them reaching the embryonic dockyard at Chatham, a little upstream.

Although urbanization changed the landscape, Upnor's immediate environment retains something of its rural feel: with the castle's conversion in 1668 for use as a powder magazine, the increasingly strict rules for explosive storage and handling ensured that it remained relatively isolated.

Above: *Map of the Medway and Thames areas, showing the position of Upnor Castle in relation to other important ordnance establishments and defences*

Facing page: *The interior of the gatehouse passage, looking west onto the causeway through one of the wickets of the entrance doors*

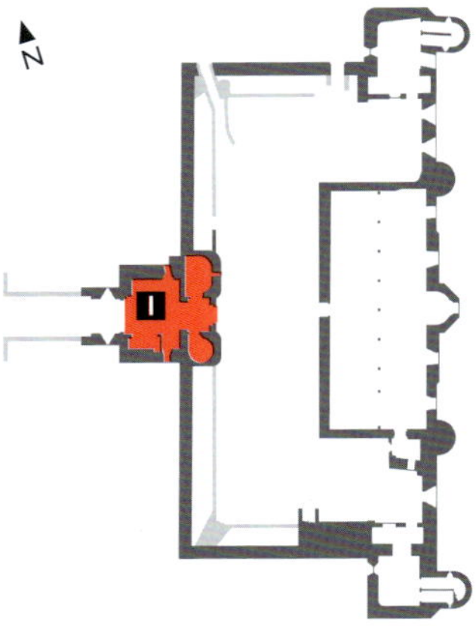

Above right: *The main entrance to the castle through the gatehouse of 1599–1601. The double doors with wickets for pedestrians are later, possibly copies of the originals*

Below: *The timber lintel in the south wall of the entrance passage bears the inscription 'W Webster XXIII Regt, 1787, May', probably the work of a bored guard*

1 GATEHOUSE

The gatehouse was the only entrance by land to the castle. It served as a checkpoint, where visitors identified themselves to the castle guards. Together with the dry ditch and courtyard wall it dates mostly from between 1599 and 1601, when Upnor was extensively modernized. Until then the landward side of the castle may have been protected only by a stout fence and timber gate.

Entrance

The entrance was originally reached via a drawbridge over the ditch, which, when first dug in 1599, was nearly 10m wide and 5.5m deep. The current causeway dates from the 18th century, though the drawbridge was probably replaced earlier than this – perhaps in the 1650s, when the roughly built walls flanking the entrance may have been added. These walls have old-fashioned cross loops, of early 16th-century design, for handguns.

The immensely solid timber outer doors incorporate two wickets (doors for pedestrian access) with handgun loops; they probably date from after the castle came under the control of the Board of Ordnance in 1668 (see page 23). Similarly the massive fireplace on the south side of the passage inside is not original, but was here by 1725, as was a small room (now gone) on the north side of the passage. In both walls of the passage are gun loops with sockets in their sills for pivots, which allowed

gunfire to be directed along the length of the west curtain wall. Their lines of fire intersected at the corners of the wall with those of gun-ports in the North and South Towers, providing continuous cover of the landward side of the castle.

The inner doors to the passage, opening onto the courtyard, were at some point reset further back to align with the east walls of the gatehouse turrets; the existing doors are late 18th century. A little room with a blocked fireplace in the north turret was probably the main guardroom. Opposite this a newel stair leads to two upper floors over the gate passage.

Upper Floors

The two upper rooms may have served as lodgings for garrison officers. Both rooms and their floor levels have been greatly altered. In 1653 a fire broke out in the gatehouse, causing major damage; the scorched red stones that can still be seen in the first-floor walls are the result of its intense heat. During the subsequent repairs in the 1650s the brick upper sections of the gatehouse were added. The extra height provided more space and, perhaps more importantly, allowed guns at roof level in the double-splayed gun-ports better command of the landward approach to the castle. Low on the second-floor walls are blocked remains of three small, splayed gun-ports and in the plaster on the inner (east) side is a crude painting of a sailing ship; the style of its rigging suggests a date of about 1700.

The original form of the east side of the upper floors is unknown; open platforms for sharpshooters may once have been supported between the turrets. The current wooden panels and balustrades date from 1951, but 18th-century prints show that similar arrangements existed here then.

The clock and its bell in the bellcote on the roof were added by the Board of Ordnance in about 1809 – the date stamped into the bell – to ensure its workers kept to time.

Above: *The gatehouse seen from the castle courtyard. The small door in the side wall probably led to a timber wall-walk behind the curtain wall*

Below: *An engraving of 1757 of Upnor Castle from the west. A sentry stands with his musket to the left of the causeway, which was still relatively new at this stage*

The Medway and the Royal Navy

From the early 16th century the new permanent Royal Navy made increasing use of the Medway.

Below: *Portrait by Marcus Gheeraerts the Younger of William Camden, 1609. Camden noted approvingly of Upnor in 1586: 'the Medway … forms a dock furnished for the finest fleet the sun ever beheld … built lately by our most gracious sovereign Elizabeth at great expense for the security of her subjects and the terror of her enemies with a fort on the shore for its defence'*

With the creation of a permanent Navy by Henry VII and Henry VIII in the early 16th century came the need for sheltered moorings for warships near suitable sites for facilities to build, maintain, repair and fit out the fleet. The safety of the anchorage was crucial, as naval operations were restricted to the summer and so warships were laid up throughout the winter months. Portsmouth had ample safe anchorages and a royal dockyard from 1492, but it was inconveniently far from the seat of government in London. A little later, warships were moored in the Thames at Deptford and Woolwich and royal dockyards established in both towns. But moorings there were limited, so the Navy began to make use of the Medway, where there were plentiful sheltered anchorages within easy reach of London.

In 1547 the Navy hired storehouses at Chatham, marking the beginnings of the dockyard. Three years later the Privy Council agreed that the waters of the Medway below Rochester Bridge were ideal for mooring warships, as were the low banks and absence of strong currents for grounding them for repairs. By 1564, of the fleet's 29 warships, 23 were moored in the Medway and only six at Portsmouth, and the Navy had a cluster of buildings, a wharf and a crane at Chatham. In 1618 it acquired more land downriver, beside the original site, where it expanded and largely rebuilt the dockyard.

Chatham was strategically located for the North Sea, and rose to be England's premier

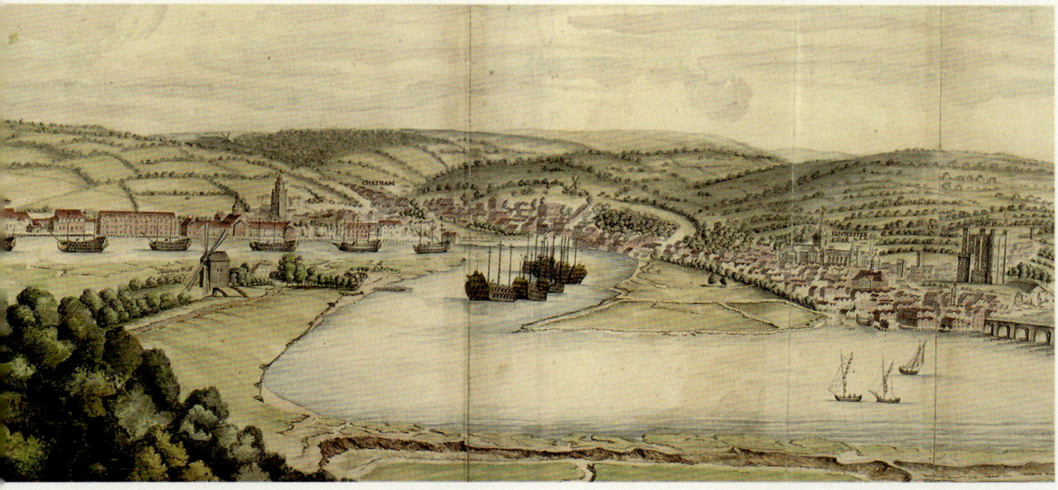

dockyard during the Dutch wars of the 17th century. In 1665 a new dockyard was founded at Sheerness, at the mouth of the Medway, to spare larger ships sailing upriver for minor repairs or to have their hulls cleaned; but its cramped and exposed location limited its growth.

In 1720 Daniel Defoe wrote of Chatham: 'The buildings here are indeed like the ships themselves, surprisingly large, and in the several kinds beautiful: the warehouses for laying up the naval treasure are the largest in dimension, and the most in number, that are anywhere to be seen in the world'. From the 1690s, as the Atlantic powers of France and Spain became England's main opponents, the Medway dockyards lost the importance they had had during the Dutch conflicts, in favour of Plymouth and Portsmouth, but remained vital for shipbuilding and repair. By the mid 18th century Chatham had become a major warship-building yard, a role it upheld into the 20th century. Between 1864 and 1885 the Admiralty again extended the dockyard, acquiring a vast swathe of land opposite Upnor: St Mary's Creek and St Mary's Island beyond it. Here it built facilities for the steam-driven metal-hulled warships then revolutionizing the world's navies. St Mary's Creek was dredged to create three huge basins and beside them engineering workshops and massive dry-docks were built.

In 1984 the dockyard, by then a full naval base, was closed and the Chatham Historic Dockyard Trust was founded to conserve the historic heart of the base and open it to visitors.

Above: *View of 1698 from the steeple of Finsbury Church towards Chatham Dockyard. Upnor Castle is shown on the far left, just beyond the slope of the hill on this side of the river, and at the far right is Rochester Castle and bridge*
Below: *View and plan of Chatham Dockyard in 1755 by Pierre-Charles Canot. Many of the buildings shown survive today and, together with the early 19th-century buildings and engineering works, form the finest and most complete example of a major dockyard of a sailing navy in the world*

Above: *Aerial view of Upnor Castle showing its main gun positions focused on the Medway*

Below: *This door, adjacent to the main building, is clad in copper to minimize the risk of sparks and is dated 1767*

2 COURTYARD

The courtyard was the hub of garrison life, the site for garrison parades and the link between the buildings. Its curtain wall was extensively rebuilt following a survey in 1623 listing necessary repairs. The storm poles (to prevent scaling the wall) along the top of the wall are inserted into sockets that would have held similar stakes and probably date from 1623; the sockets were discovered in 1974. Along the base of the wall on the inner side are the brick footings of lean-to storerooms. They were built probably in the 18th century, as were the passage with its curious brick oven in the north-west corner and the drain in the south-west corner. The arched opening in the wall beside the North Tower was probably built in about 1810 to provide a shortcut between the main building (by then a magazine) and the new ordnance facilities just north of the castle.

The circular well to the north is close to what was the kitchen in the main building. At the other end of the main building, on its south wall, is a scar in the stonework where a shoe room stood in the 18th century. Here, to minimize the risk of sparks causing an explosion, munitions workers changed from their hobnailed boots into special slippers before entering the building. The adjacent copper-clad door bears the initials and date 'GR 1767' (for *Georgius Rex*, George III), in copper nails. This door leads to a stair to the water bastion.

In its final use between about 1860 and 1920 as a proof yard for testing gunpowder samples, the courtyard had lawns and flower beds. The Turkey oak is a survivor of a pair reputedly grown from acorns brought back from the Crimean War (1853–6). In front of the main building are two water tanks dated 1856 with their Board of Ordnance coats of arms.

TOWERS

The existing North and South Towers date mainly from 1599–1601. They were built over the remains of the towers of the original castle of 1559–67, as designed by Sir Richard Lee, and incorporate the half-round turrets of these first towers on the river frontage. Lee's turrets appear to survive to the string course at first-floor level and have 'dumb-bell' and 'keyhole' firing loops; inside are his stairs and latrines with contemporary door frames. Little else is known about Lee's towers, which may simply have supported gun platforms above the top of the river bank.

The extended two-storey towers of 1599–1601 created three gun platforms, one of which was at roof level. The new towers, like the contemporary gatehouse, were built of neat, squared, coursed rubble. Originally they may have been open-backed, like wall towers in some medieval castles. At the base of the west wall of each tower are the remains of a gun-port; these allowed cover of the short lengths of the courtyard wall. Each tower is linked to the main building by a short length of curtain wall containing three gun embrasures; their parapets were raised in 1601 and again in the 18th century.

In the mid 17th century the towers were adapted to form garrison lodgings. Probably some time after 1668, when the castle was converted into a powder magazine, the gun-ports were mostly blocked or turned into windows, and each tower extended in brick and made habitable. Later, both roof-level gun platforms were replaced by a third floor. Neither tower would have made especially comfortable quarters. Possibly they were occupied by the officers in charge of the magazine guards until the building of the barracks in 1718.

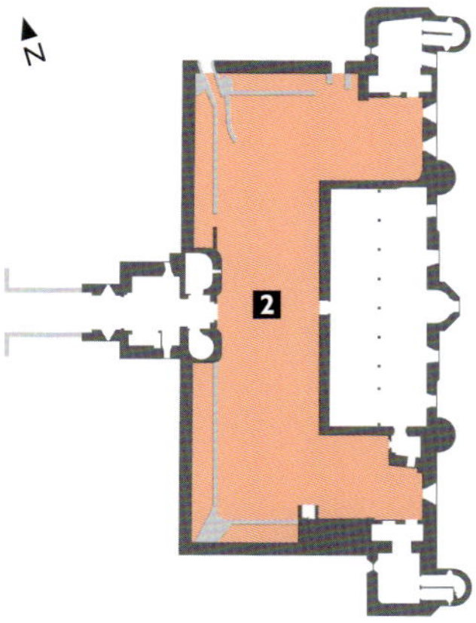

Below: *Looking downriver from the water bastion. Along the bank are former ordnance stores of the 19th century. The scar on the castle wall shows the outline of the 'shifting house', where gun powder was unloaded and inspected*

Above: Upnor Castle from the river Medway. Its wooded setting is a legacy of the need to keep powder magazines isolated from other buildings in case of fire or explosion

Below: The passage behind the water bastion, which linked the bastion to the new ordnance facilities immediately north of the castle

3 South Tower

We know little about the use of either tower after the castle's conversion for use as a magazine. But Edward Hasted noted in his great *History and Topographical Survey of the County of Kent* (1778–99) that, 'The south tower of Upnor Castle is allowed to the Governor for his house, at which, on account of its unfitness for his reception, he never resides'. In about 1800 the South Tower became a laboratory where shells and cartridges were filled with gunpowder, ammunition was repaired, and gunpowder of different strengths was mixed for naval use, purposes reflected in the surviving copper sheathing on doors and the internal shutters here. The external brick steps to the first floor may have been added during this time. For much of the 20th century the tower was probably used for storage.

4 North Tower

No details of the North Tower's inhabitants are known, but by the 1770s a cooperage (where barrels are made) occupied the space between the tower and the north wall of the main building. The mark of its gable is visible above the entrance to the tower. The cooperage survived until the late 19th century, inconveniently restricting access to the tower except through it and almost certainly limiting the tower to storage use.

In 1806, during the Napoleonic Wars, the tower rooms held an assortment of ordnance stores. The basement (not open) contained unserviceable gunpowder stored for later remixing. Ammunition was kept on the ground floor and what were probably Congreve rockets (a type of missile invented in 1804) and blue signal lights on the floor above. The top floor held lumber. The tower seems to have been used for miscellaneous stores at intervals well into the 20th century.

5 MAIN BUILDING

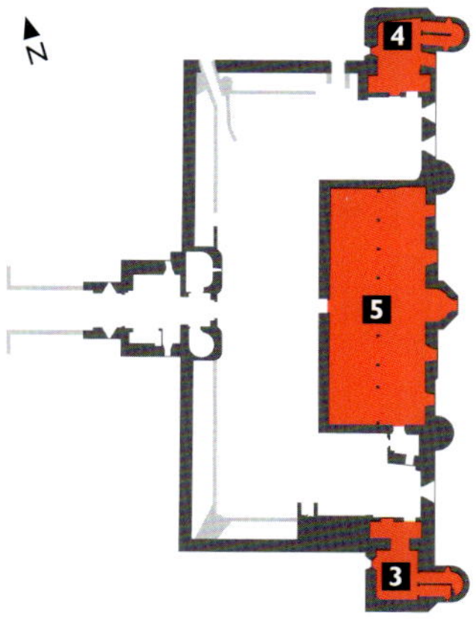

Between the towers, behind the water bastion, stands the two-storey rectangular main building of the castle of 1559–67. It originally served as garrison accommodation and stores, with a kitchen and dining room noted in the building accounts. When the building was converted into a huge powder magazine in 1668 it was so altered that its original overall appearance is not certain, although some details are known.

Above its entrance from the courtyard are the remains of a stone plaque that would have borne the arms of Elizabeth I. As first built, this entrance opened onto a central passage, flanked by two large ground-floor rooms, leading directly ahead to stairs down to the water bastion. Along the riverfront the space between the outer wall of the main building and the now-vanished heightened revetment wall within the main building formed a firing gallery. The first floor may have been arranged on a similar plan; the blocked remains of an original fireplace here date from the intended use of the building as garrison accommodation. The riverfront had loops or narrow windows for handguns; traces survive of these openings. Building accounts for work in 1601 suggest that heavy weapons were mounted on platforms at roof level.

On the riverfront a number of original Tudor doorways with four-centred heads (low, wide arches with pointed apexes) survive at bastion level.

Powder Magazine

The blocked rectangular mullioned windows on the riverfront and on the first floor overlooking the courtyard date from the conversion of 1668, as do the distinctive roundels, the large round-headed windows on the stair turret and the ornamental battlements on the riverfront shown in a 1698 drawing (below).

Below: *Elevation of Upnor Castle drawn in 1698. Due to the angle of the view the storekeeper's brick and tiled house is shown to the right of the castle; its correct position when seen face on is to the left*

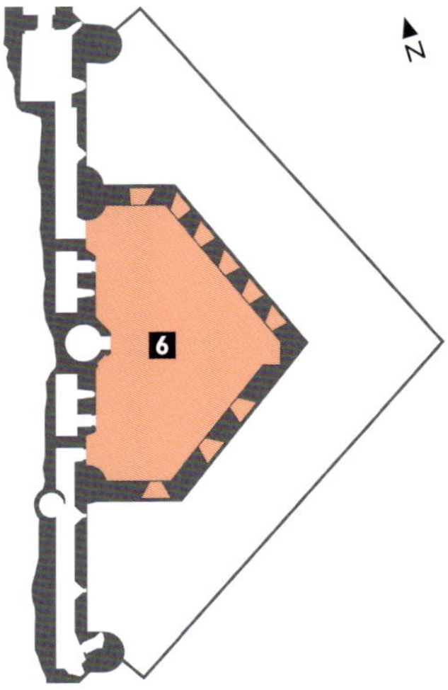

Right: The ground floor of the main building, with replica powder barrels on racks. Originally barrels would have been stacked almost to ceiling height

Below: View downriver from the water bastion. The two guns here are 24-pounders dredged from St Mary's Creek in 1876. They are thought to be from the Charles V or the Matthias, former Dutch warships captured early in the Anglo-Dutch wars and added to the English fleet. Both ships were burned and sunk by the Dutch during the Medway raid in 1667

Just above the lower line of roundels the masonry changes to larger, less regular rubble, indicating the extensive 1668 rebuilding. This change can be seen elsewhere on the building at this level.

A 1725 plan of the interior shows two powder magazines occupying the positions of the ground-floor rooms, suggesting survival of the original internal layout here. This was swept away later in the 18th century to create, on each floor, a single large powder store. The substantial wall that had supported the rear of the first-floor gun platforms was demolished to ground level and the roof was probably rebuilt at this time and extended to the riverfront wall. The woodblock ground floor, the copper-clad doors and internal shutters, which may be later, and the absence of ironwork all reflect magazine use and the need to minimize the risk of sparks.

6 WATER BASTION, 1559–67

When the castle was built the riverbank was fronted with a substantial stone revetment wall, which formed the rear of the water bastion below the ground level of the main castle site. The main building was then built to oversail the riverbank and revetment wall, with its riverfront wall built up in front of it from the water bastion. The narrow space between these two parallel walls, at water-bastion level, was used as a passage to the North and South Towers and for storage. At ground level the revetment wall was stepped back some 2m. Its original height above ground level is not known but its most likely purpose was as the rear support for timber gun platforms commanding the river at first-floor level on either side of the central stair turret of the main building.

The water bastion is best reached via the central spiral stair. It is one of the earliest artillery bastions in Britain, its original lower levels and gun platform still extant, and a rarity on an artillery fort for being a solitary feature. Usually, bastions projected at intervals in front of the ramparts of a fortress to provide covering fire. Here, the architect, Sir Richard Lee, may have used this solo bastion to allow guns on the north to fire at hostile warships approaching up the Medway and those on the south to engage any smaller craft aiming to bypass Upnor via St Mary's Creek and emerge a little upriver.

The bastion and its parapets were raised in height during the 1599–1601 works, by which time rounded parapets, designed to deflect incoming shot, but having proved not very successful at it, were going out of fashion. The present six embrasures facing downstream and three facing upstream probably mirror the Tudor layout.

On either side of the door to the stair turret two doors lead to small chambers, dating from the first building of the castle, which probably held munitions and equipment for the bastion guns. To the south another door leads to the passage to the South Tower basement. Its counterpart to the North Tower was widened and the passage extended to link the bastion to the ordnance yard developing just outside the castle to the north in the early 19th century.

Above these doors are the corbels and roofline of the shifting house and laboratories built by the Board of Ordnance in the late 18th and early 19th centuries. Munitions were offloaded here from a timber jetty projecting from the tip of the bastion. The timber palisade round the water bastion replaces at least one earlier one built to deter raiders approaching from the river or along the shore at low tide.

Below: *Plan of Upnor Castle drawn in 1725. At this date the main building, although used as a powder magazine, still retained its original internal layout*

Bottom: *JMW Turner's painting of about 1831 gives a vivid impression of the Medway crowded with warships and overlooked by Upnor Castle and its barracks. On the hill on the left are the Chatham Lines guarding the landward approach to Chatham Dockyard*

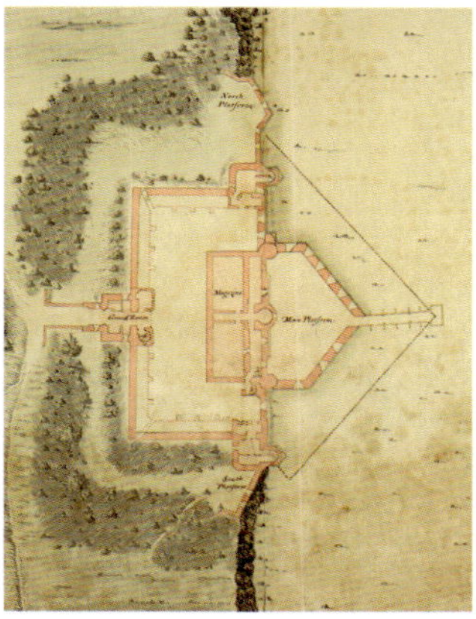

Above: *Upnor in 1793 by Samuel Ireland, who made this sketch sheltering from the wind in a boat beneath the stern of a man-of-war. Sailors row a cutter past what may be a powder boat beside the water bastion with its shifting house and powder jetty. To the left are a couple of small gun vessels*

Below: *This capstan, dating from 1826/7, was used to raise powder barrels from the water bastion to the first floor of the magazine*

Right: *The castle in 1862, its use overshadowed by the two huge magazines of 1808 and 1856, a shell store and laboratories*

The Castle Becomes a Powder Magazine

The main castle building was converted in 1668 from garrison living quarters into a store for gunpowder – many thousands of barrels of powder were kept here.

Until its abolition in 1855 the Board of Ordnance provided all gunpowder for the Army and Navy. It came at first from private merchants and manufacturers, notably the East India Company. But increasing dissatisfaction with its quality led the Board in 1759 to buy and operate a powder works at Faversham and another in 1787 at Waltham Abbey, where powder and other explosives were manufactured on a huge scale into the late 20th century.

Powder was transported and stored in wooden barrels, each usually holding about 40kg.

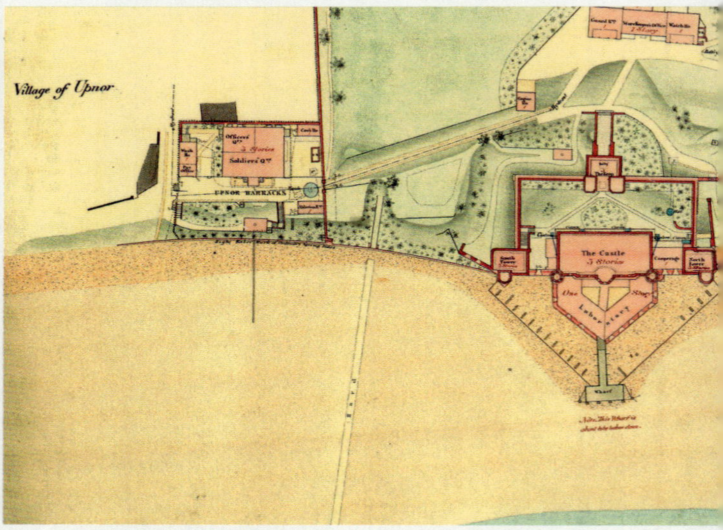

At first these were shipped to Chatham from London merchants, the Tower of London and other ordnance magazines on the Thames. Some powder was probably stored at Chatham on Gun Wharf, founded by the Board in 1656 at the south end of the dockyard. From there the barrels were issued to fortifications and to warships at the dockyard, or at Sheerness or its off-lying anchorage of the Nore (a sandbank about 4.5 miles long at the mouth of the Medway; see map on page 3). Warships entering Chatham Dockyard for repairs, or being decommissioned, would in turn unload their powder and return it to the ordnance stores.

Until the early 18th century, when large, specialized powder magazines to broadly standard designs were developed by the Board of Ordnance, gunpowder was stored in a variety of buildings. It needed dry, cool, well-ventilated and secure storage, preferably in an isolated location in case of fire or explosion. Upnor had the merits of relative isolation, defensive design and proximity to the river for transporting supplies, and in 1668 was converted to ordnance use.

A jetty was added to the water bastion to allow powder boats to moor alongside. By the end of the 18th century the bastion was covered by a single-storey building known as a shifting house, where powder was inspected after being unloaded from the boats. Both powder and barrels were examined to check they were serviceable and stable. The barrels were then hoisted to the magazine and stacked in timber-framed storage bays on both floors.

A 1750 inspection of Upnor by the Surveyor General (the official in charge of the building and engineering section of the Board of Ordnance) revealed much amiss, as well as an attitude to safety very different from that of today. After commenting adversely on the 'great disorder' and 'want of neatness and regularity everywhere', he noted how the 90lb powder barrels reached the magazine: 'The method now used to lift up the powder barrels into the magazine is by running a rope through a pulley, one end of which is fastened to a powder barrel, and a man taking hold of the other jumps out of the window, and his weight draws up the barrel into the magazine, which is a dangerous and uncertain method, for if he is too light, the powder barrel will not ascend, and if he is too heavy, he is sure to bruise himself against the pavement, whereby it is very difficult to get men who will run such a risk upon labourer's pay'.

The solution was to install a pulley worked by a capstan (a winding machine like a windlass, but rotated parallel to the ground rather than at right angles); the capstan at Upnor is contemporary with the spiral stairs, which were remodelled in 1826/7.

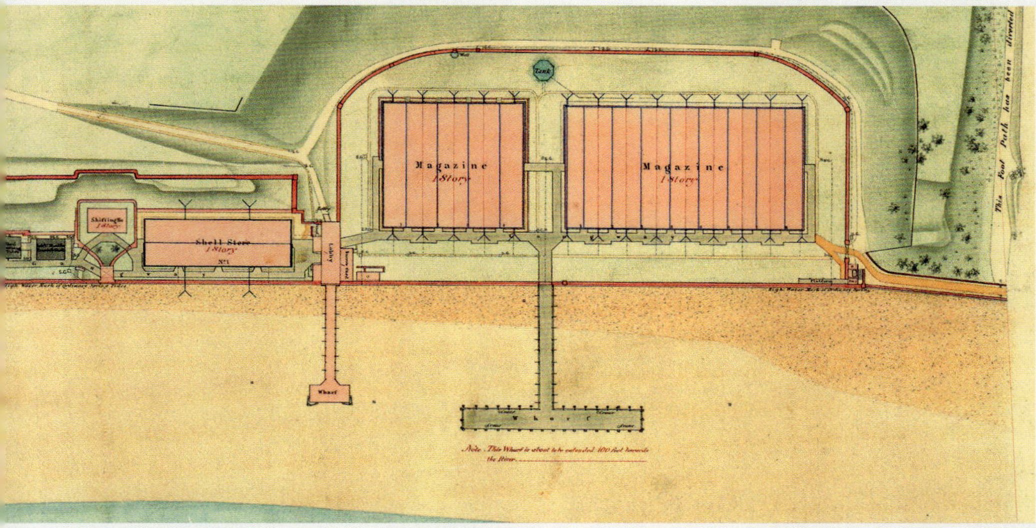

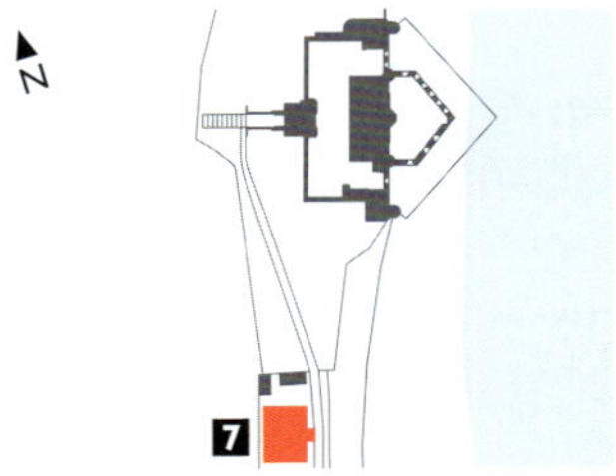

Below: One of the first-floor rooms of Upnor Barracks, built in 1718 and little altered since then, except for the insertion of a cast-iron fireplace in the 19th century

Bottom: The barracks stand at the end of Upnor High Street, overlooking the river Medway. In the distance are the roofs of the immense 19th-century building slips where ships were built and repaired under cover at Chatham Dockyard

7 BARRACKS

Upnor Barracks, one of the oldest and least-altered Army barracks in the country, was built in 1718. At that time permanent forces were largely limited to the king's foot and horse guards based in London, and to small groups of gunners and soldiers guarding coastal and other defences. Many of the men would have been billeted with the local community, as probably happened at Upnor between 1668 and completion of the barracks. Purpose-designed barracks, then a relatively new concept, were intended to replace billeting, which was unpopular with local communities and bad for discipline.

The barracks has three main storeys and an attic. It accommodated two officers and their families in separate quarters in the rear half of the building. The fireplaces and wooden pegs for hanging soldiers' kit date from the 19th century. The front half was probably designed to house between 64 and 80 soldiers in much less spacious conditions. Postings here could be for many years. The occupants lived, slept, cooked and ate in these rooms. The single-storey buildings across the small courtyards at each end of the barracks housed privies and limited washing facilities. A cookhouse was added north of the barracks before 1846.

A rare 1795 inspection report reveals overcrowded conditions of Hogarthian squalor here: 'some of the rooms of only about 17 feet square having no less than 18 men besides many women and children quartered in them, whereas they are calculated for no more than ten men'. Although conditions improved, in the 1850s mortality rates in Army accommodation were almost twice as high as those in equivalent civilian lodgings. Upnor Barracks was closed soon afterwards and subsequently used for various purposes, including for stores and workshops. The first-floor barrack rooms may be visited.

Left: *A depiction of life in an English barracks, by Thomas Rowlandson, 1791. Such cramped conditions, lacking in any privacy, were no doubt familiar at Upnor*

Below: *Clay tobacco pipe (1730–40) probably used by the castle guards. Smoking was strictly forbidden near the magazine*

Garrison Life

Until the barracks were built in about 1718, the men were billeted with the local community or slept in the castle itself.

Little is known of the men of the castle garrison during its life as a fortress until 1668. Artillery fortifications then were among very few places where soldiers were employed by the Crown in peacetime. The Office of Ordnance (see page 23) was responsible for the numbers and competence of the men and for the supply of weapons, ammunition, uniforms, rations, lodgings, beds and bedding. The men lodged in the main building, sleeping several to a bed; as at other forts, some had wives and families and would have lodged outside the castle, most likely in Upnor village.

During peacetime the castle was generally guarded by a small, caretaker garrison. Records show, for instance, that in 1588 there was a master gunner and six gunners, and in 1603 and 1623 there was a master gunner, paid 1s. 4*d.* a day, seven gunners, paid 1s., and 20 soldiers, paid 8*d.* During wartime such numbers were supplemented, as in 1596, when Lord Admiral Howard complained of the inadequacy of the garrison, which was hastily increased to 80 men. Their pay of 8*d.* – roughly that of a farmworker – indicates they were ordinary soldiers.

By the 18th century most regiments allowed sergeants and about seven per cent of soldiers to marry. Once on the regiment's Married Roll they could live in barracks. On campaign, the women often acted as nurses and orderlies. At a backwater like Upnor, where men could be stationed for years, out of sight of high authority, it is unlikely the rules were strictly adhered to.

Peacetime garrison life would have been uneventful and at times monotonous, centred on guard duties and gun drill. But with government money lacking, the castle and its equipment were often in poor repair. The 1623 inventory recorded only 8lb of gunpowder in store – less than a tenth of a barrel.

After Upnor became a powder store in 1668, the quality of men forming the guard sometimes caused concern. In 1745 the storekeeper (in charge of the magazine) complained to the castle governor: 'I am of the opinion that we have not a sufficient number of men to guard so material a place and that what we have are so very bad by their being very antient and seldom sober that they are not fit to be trusted here.'

The following February, after part of the riverbank below the barracks collapsed, the same storekeeper requested that a temporary fence should be erected to prevent the soldiers 'who are a sett of drunken wretches' from falling over the bank.

Saint maris
Haw
Cokam wode
Barow hil
West march
Saint marikrike
Toyarbil
Gillingam
West·courte
Chattam
Gillingam·parsonag
Saint margats
Long port

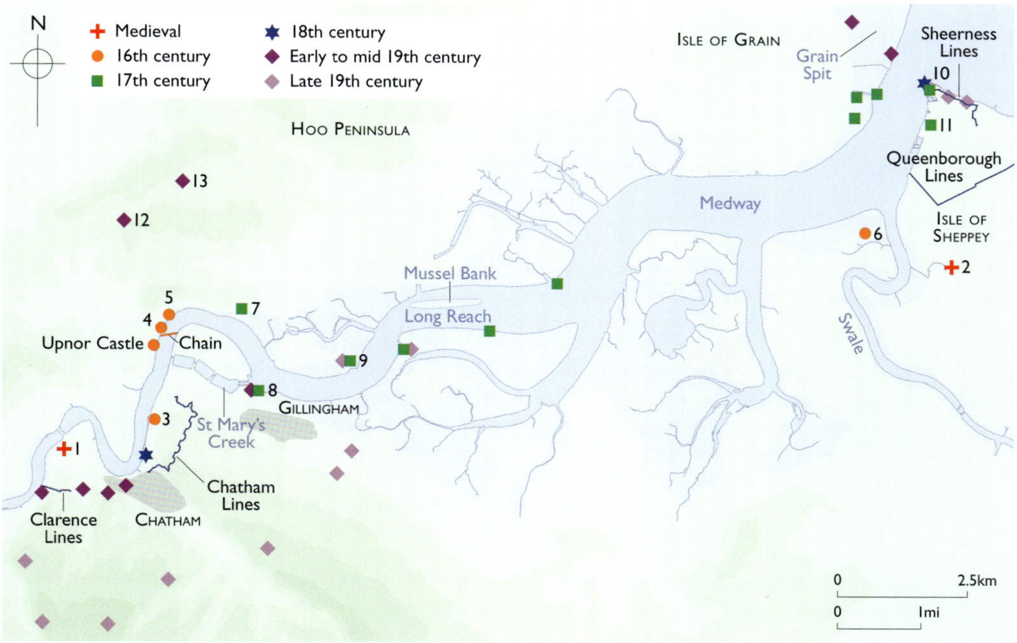

History of Upnor Castle

THE BUILDING OF UPNOR CASTLE, 1559–67

Upnor Castle was begun in 1559 during the reign of Elizabeth I (r.1558–1603) in response to developments in military technology then revolutionizing warfare. Increasingly powerful guns had been made from the beginning of the century. At sea this led to the development of specialized vessels – warships such as the *Mary Rose*, armed with broadsides of guns – and the establishment by the early Tudor kings of a permanent Royal Navy. Such warships needed repairs, regular maintenance and safe anchorages when not in use. Increasingly, the Navy made use of the sheltered waters of the Medway, leading to the development of Chatham Dockyard just a little upriver of the site where Upnor Castle would be built.

In 1558 Elizabeth inherited with her crown a substantial navy that was a continual drain on her finances. But she also faced the enmity of Catholic France and Spain, so maintaining a strong navy and protection for her fleet bases was a priority. Upnor Castle was sited to prevent raiders venturing upriver from reaching Chatham, which was rapidly becoming England's main fleet anchorage, with its embryonic dockyard. Significantly, when built, Upnor's garrison (comprising eight gunners initially) was put under naval control; more usually a local member of the county establishment would have been appointed captain and would have recruited local men to mount a garrison.

Above: *Map of the Medway defences*

1 *Rochester Castle*
2 *Queenborough Castle*
3 *Chatham Dockyard*
4 *Bay Sconce*
5 *Warham Sconce*
6 *Swaleness Fort*
7 *Cockham Wood Fort*
8 *Gillingham Fort*
9 *Hoo Ness Battery*
10 *Sheerness Fort*
11 *Sheerness Dockyard*
12 *Chattenden Magazine*
13 *Lodge Hill Magazine*

Facing page: *Detail of a chart of the course of the Medway from Rochester to the Nore. It shows clearly what a major anchorage the Medway had become for the Navy by the time this was drawn, in 1585. Upnor Castle is depicted beside the northernmost ships of the queen's fleet*

Architects and Design

Upnor's design, conceived when the architecture of fortifications was rapidly evolving, is unique.

Facing page: *Proposed coastal fortifications at Orwell Haven, Essex, drawn by Sir Richard Lee in 1543. These were never built but in the design of the lower blockhouse Lee incorporates two embryonic bastions of similar shape to his later water bastion at Upnor Castle*

The design and building of Upnor were the responsibility of Sir Richard Lee, a military engineer with extensive experience in both studying and building artillery fortifications in England and English-controlled Calais. When Upnor was built, however, much of Lee's energy was devoted to fortifying Portsmouth and to his great bastioned defences at Berwick, so his involvement with Upnor was largely limited to drawing the plan and advising on the necessary skills of the builders. His deputy, Humphrey Locke, described as overseer, surveyor and chief carpenter, was more closely involved. But the man with the greatest responsibility for the work was Richard Watts, who acted as the local administrator and paymaster of the labour force. Watts was a major government contractor, supplying victuals to the Army and Navy. Later he was MP and Mayor of Rochester, where he founded almshouses that still bear his name.

Upnor's design, conceived by Lee when the architecture of artillery fortifications was rapidly

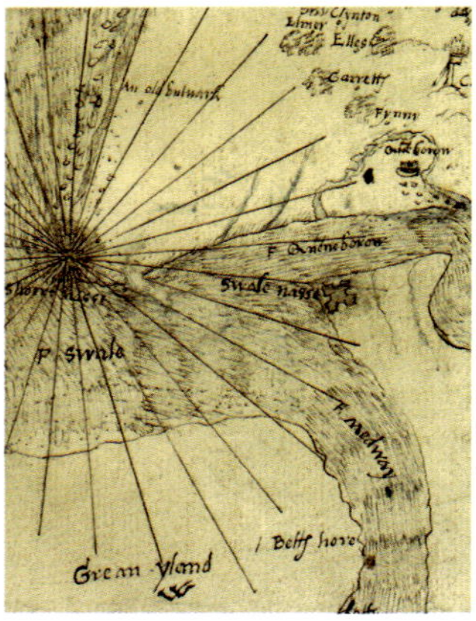

Above: *Detail of a map of the Isle of Sheppey drawn in 1574 and thought to be the work of the cartographer Robert Lythe. It shows Sir William Winter's proposed fort at Swaleness, as well as Queenborough Castle*

WAR WITH SPAIN, 1588–1604

War with Spain, although it began in 1585, was not openly declared until after the execution of Mary, Queen of Scots, in 1587, which led to outrage in Catholic Europe and gave the Spanish king Philip II the excuse to invade England. This Philip attempted in 1588, in the guise of a Catholic crusade.

Years of strained relations before then, however, had aroused English fears that the fleet anchorage and embryonic naval base at Chatham would be the target of raids from Spanish-controlled ports in the Low Countries. So in 1575, following recommendations by the experienced and highly competent Surveyor of the Navy, Sir William Winter, the site for a fort was prepared downriver at Swaleness opposite Queenborough Castle (although subsequently abandoned as unsuitable). Winter also recommended that docking facilities be built for warships at Queenborough rather than at Chatham, presumably because of Queenborough's closer proximity to the sea; but perhaps for that reason it was considered vulnerable to attack and the idea was dropped. At the same time timber piles were used to block St Mary's Creek, immediately downriver of Chatham and opposite Upnor Castle, to prevent the existing naval anchorage being attacked in the flank. A few years later William Bourne, who was master gunner at Upnor in 1579/80, recommended that a boom, or chain, be secured across the river to stop enemy

evolving, is unique. Its solitary bastion is paralleled only by one at Milton Blockhouse at Gravesend, built in 1539 and altered by Lee in 1545. For town defences the future lay with massive bastioned ramparts able to withstand bombardment, such as at Berwick and later at Chatham, in the great 18th-century defences surrounding the dockyard known as the Lines. Smaller fortifications against warships varied from simple earthwork gun batteries to more elaborate bastioned masonry defences.

Upnor's angled water bastion, possibly deriving from Lee's very different land bastions of 1558 at Berwick, enabled guns to cover the river approaches downstream and upstream, but proved woefully inadequate during the Dutch attack in 1667. Behind and above the water bastion on the riverbank the main building provided quarters for the garrison and additional gun positions at two levels.

warships. He considered such a defence likely to be more effective than the castle's guns, which he thought would simply damage sails and rigging. When war with Spain broke out in 1585 a chain was installed but, as the size of the fleet grew and further moorings were needed near Chatham, it was later moved downriver and so beyond the protection of the castle. Probably at the same time two gun batteries – Bay Sconce and Warham Sconce (later rebuilt as James's, or Middleton, Battery and Bird's Nest Battery respectively) – were built on the north bank downriver of Upnor to cover the extended moorings. Records of Upnor's garrison and its armament are fragmentary. In the Armada year of 1588 its body of trained artillerymen consisted of a master gunner and six gunners; undoubtedly there was also a number of soldiers. Whether over the next eight years this garrison shrunk, or remained the same, is not known, but in 1596 the Lord Admiral and head of the Navy, Charles, Lord Howard of Effingham, later 1st Earl of Nottingham, considered it so inadequate he recommended that it should be either properly manned or demolished to prevent it falling into enemy hands. He suggested 50 trained men were needed; a month later it had a garrison of 80 (probably a mix of gunners and soldiers). In 1603, after the castle's modernization, it mounted some 20 weapons of varying calibres, while Bay Sconce had four guns and the larger Warham Sconce had seven.

Below: *Lord Howard of Effingham by Daniel Mytens, c.1620. During the war with Spain, Howard urged an enlargement of Upnor's garrison; earlier he had admonished the queen for underrating the Spanish threat: 'For the love of Jesus Christ, Madam, awake thoroughly, and see the villainous treasons round about you'*

Right: *The main elevation of the castle from the water bastion. Properly supplied and armed, and with a determined garrison, the strengthened castle of 1601, with its tiers of defences, was a potentially formidable obstacle*

Below: *Solid cast-iron shot, found just north of the castle; such shot was the mainstay of artillery from the 15th century to the mid 19th century, when it was replaced by shells*

WORKS AT THE CASTLE, 1599–1601

By the 1590s, with the Navy's increasing use of the Medway and war with Spain, it was imperative to strengthen Upnor. In October 1599 Sir John Leveson, a former soldier and deputy lieutenant for Kent, was asked to organize the work and made paymaster. The military engineers responsible for the design were Baptista (about whom nothing more is known) and Arthur Gregory, who also oversaw the building work. Gregory had an unusual career that included making musical instruments, designing fireships (ships set alight and sent among the enemy fleet to spread fire and confusion) and surveying. Acting for Sir Francis Walsingham, Elizabeth I's Secretary of State, he had also intercepted and copied the confidential correspondence of Mary, Queen of Scots, when she was Elizabeth's prisoner.

The works at Upnor soon exceeded the estimates, but the building accounts show that significant weaknesses in the design were remedied. To impede enemies storming the castle from the river a stout timber palisade was built on the foreshore in front of the water bastion. The bastion itself was raised and the existing 'parapet of good height … with loops for great ordnance' was built. 'The tymber platforms on bothe sides of the tower to be new made and covered with lead' almost certainly refers to renewal of gun platforms flanking the top of the stair tower linking the bastion to the main building. The scant landward defences were addressed: a curtain wall was built to enclose the courtyard and main building (replacing what may simply have been a wooden fence), surrounded by a dry ditch nearly 10m wide and 5.5m deep. A new well 'six fathoms deep' (11m) may refer to the one surviving today; an earlier well stood somewhere outside the castle.

The towers were largely rebuilt, being raised to two storeys, with rooftop gun platforms overlooking the river and ground-floor gun-ports to cover the short arms of the ditch. The parapets on the walls linking each tower to the main building were raised. The gatehouse was built at the centre of the new curtain wall to the west, with a gun-port on each side of its ground floor to cover the ditch. The accounts list 'making the drawbridge with iron chains and an engine [windlass] to raise it'. Building material was requisitioned or bought from various local sources. As when the castle was first built, much of the stone was salvaged from the abandoned Rochester Castle. By the autumn of 1601 the work was largely complete.

Above: *The Parliamentarian general Sir Thomas Fairfax by Wenceslaus Hollar in 1648, the year that Fairfax visited Upnor during the Civil War*

Below: *A hefty brass-bound lock on display in the museum and said to be the original gatehouse lock of 1599–1601. Note the broad arrow and the 'O' of the Board of Ordnance marked in the wood*

REPAIRS AND CIVIL WAR, 1600–1653

James I (r.1603–25) and Charles I (r.1625–49) had little money to spare for defences and Upnor, as many other fortifications, fell into disrepair. The 1623 survey stated that the drawbridge and its mechanism were broken, a number of gun platforms needed to be replaced, and much of the courtyard wall had collapsed. There was still a garrison, but with only 18 guns and limited powder and shot, compared to the 20 guns here in 1603. Archaic, but still useful, weapons listed include 34 longbows and 83 sheaves (bundles of about 24) of arrows.

On the outbreak of the Civil War in 1642 Upnor and its two sconces were garrisoned by Parliamentary forces and the castle used as a prison for Royalist officers. During the Royalist uprising in Kent in 1648 the castle was seized – probably with little resistance, as no record survives of a battle – and briefly held by Royalists. After the suppression of the uprising the Parliamentary general Sir Thomas Fairfax visited and further repairs and improvements to the castle were authorized, including renewing gun platforms on the North and South Towers and probably two on the main building. In 1653, after a serious fire in the gatehouse, it was repaired and heightened in brick. At the same time a brick wall was added to the open back of the North Tower to create living quarters; the South Tower was similarly enclosed at much the same time.

Board of Ordnance

The Office of Ordnance, renamed the Board of Ordnance in 1671, evolved from two groups of officials in the royal household responsible by 1300 for providing weapons and armour for the king's military campaigns. Following the development by the early 16th century of firearms and guns, Henry VIII reorganized his officials to focus on the supply of these new weapons and ammunition to the Army, the Navy and land fortifications. Armour rapidly declined in importance. In the early 17th century the post of Master General of Ordnance was created to oversee the Board, which now employed military engineers responsible for fortifications.

In 1855 the Board was abolished, partly because of shortcomings in the Crimean War, and its responsibilities were transferred to the War Office. By the 1880s Admiralty and War Office ordnance requirements were diverging as warships' guns grew in size and complexity and were increasingly mounted in turrets. In 1891 the Admiralty's Naval Ordnance Store Department was created, acquiring depots such as Upnor that mainly supplied the fleet.

Above: *Jan van Leyden's colourful portrayal (1667–9) of the raid on the Medway, with Dutch fireships attacking two English warships (centre and right) and the Dutch flag flying over a fanciful depiction of the captured fort at Sheerness*

Below: *Admiral Michiel de Ruyter (1607–76), by Ferdinand Bol in 1667. 'De Ruyter' (from the old Dutch for 'raider') was probably a nickname he adopted, and was given to him before his raid on the Medway, when he was a successful privateer*

THE DUTCH RAID, 1667

The 1667 raid on the Medway was an extraordinary display of Dutch seamanship, courage and daring, and a humiliation for England. It followed ruthless worldwide commercial rivalry between the Netherlands and England, and the resulting war of 1652–4 and outbreak of a second in 1665, both fought largely at sea. By the end of 1666, expense and war-weariness led to peace negotiations. Charles II (r.1660–85), desperately short of money, elected not to fit out the main fleet for 1667, gambling that the Dutch would not break the unofficial truce. But the Dutch, determined to negotiate from strength, and seeking revenge for Admiral Holmes's destruction the previous summer of a Dutch merchant fleet in the Vlie estuary and brutal burning of the town of West-Terschelling, assembled a powerful fleet under their outstanding Admiral de Ruyter to raid the Thames and Medway.

The arrival off the Kent coast of de Ruyter's force of some 80 warships on 5 June 1667 caused consternation. But the Dutch lacked knowledge of the local defences and their initial foray into the Thames was halted below Gravesend. However, on 10 June they took and largely destroyed the partly built dockyard and fort at Sheerness. Upriver lay Chatham Dockyard and most of the English fleet, protected only by Upnor Castle and a chain across the Medway below Gillingham.

On 11 June the Duke of Albemarle arrived to organize defences at Upnor and Chatham, but time, men and munitions were lacking. Three blockships were hastily sunk in the river at the Mussel Bank but failed to obstruct Dutch warships skilfully navigated upriver later that day, or further reinforcements arriving the next morning. To protect Chatham and the warships beyond, Albemarle sent additional supplies to Upnor's commander, Sir Edward Scott, and installed eight guns downriver in either the abandoned Bay or Warham Sconce.

Left: *George Monck painted by Sir Peter Lely in 1665–6, at the start of the Second Dutch War, during which he was one of the two commanders of the Royal Navy*

George Monck (1608–70)

The career of George Monck, Duke of Albemarle, Army and Naval officer, vividly illustrates the conflicting loyalties and difficult decisions faced by many Englishmen in the divisive years of the mid 17th century, during the Civil War and its aftermath. Monck fought for Charles I, but was captured and in 1646 agreed to command Parliamentary forces in Ireland, later serving with Oliver Cromwell in Scotland.

On the outbreak of the First Dutch War in 1652, during the Commonwealth, he was made General-at-Sea, one of three outstanding commanders in charge of the Navy. In 1654 he suppressed a Royalist rebellion in Scotland and took charge of the country but, after Cromwell's heir was deposed by the Army and the restoration of the monarchy looked inevitable, he switched sides again and in 1660 played a key role in the return of Charles II, who made him Duke of Albemarle.

In 1666 he was appointed joint commander of the Royal Navy during the Second Dutch War (1665–7). His experience, organizational abilities and ruthless drive were invaluable in confronting the Dutch attack, but he faced formidable problems: arriving at Chatham Dockyard on 11 June he 'found scarce twelve of eight hundred men which were then in the king's pay, in his Majesty's yards; and these so distracted with fear that I could have little or no service from them'.

Nevertheless, Albemarle's actions mounting additional guns and sending supplies to Upnor helped persuade the Dutch to end their attack.

Across the river he mounted about 50 guns, including 10 from the artillery train sent from the Tower of London.

Initially the chain, guard ships and two gun batteries downriver halted the Dutch. But on 12 June Captain Jan van Brakel, in an outstandingly courageous action, sailed his small 40-gun *Vrede* through a hail of fire, capturing a guard ship and enabling a nearby Dutch fireship to break the chain. Continuing upriver the Dutch captured the flagship *Royal Charles* and burned or drove ashore other English vessels before anchoring downriver of Upnor that evening. At about midday the next day they resumed their attack. Their larger warships, forbidden to navigate up the narrowing river beyond (continued page 28)

Below: *Stern carving, c.1666, of the English flagship the* Royal Charles, *which was seized by the Dutch during the raid of the Medway*

Above: *John Evelyn (1620–1706), by Robert Walker c.1648–56. Evelyn witnessed the Dutch raid from a hill overlooking the Medway*
Right: *Evelyn's sketch of the raid, which he sent to Samuel Pepys in January 1668*

Accounts of the Dutch Raid

Two diarists recorded the events: one as news reached him in London, the other from beside the Medway.

Samuel Pepys, the noted diarist and one of the Navy's greatest and most able administrators, wrote in shock on 12 and 13 June 1667, as news of the Dutch raid reached London:

... for the newes is true, that the Dutch have broke the chaine and burned our ships ... [the people] cry out that the office of the Ordnance hath been so backward as no powder to have been at Chatham nor Upnor Castle till such a time, and the carriages all broken ... that Upnor, the good old castle built by Queen Elizabeth, should be lately slighted ... my neighbour ... tells me that he come from Chatham this evening at five o'clock, and saw this afternoon the Royall James, Oake, and London burnt by the enemy with their fire-ships; that two or three men-of-war came up with them, and made no more of Upnor castle's shooting them than of a fly.

On 20 January 1668 Pepys's friend and fellow diarist John Evelyn sent him a sketch (above)

Above: *Samuel Pepys (1633–1703) by John Hayls, c.1666. The famous diarist recorded news of the Dutch raid as it reached him in London*
Below: *Depiction of the Dutch raid by Willem Schellinks, c.1667–8. An inaccurate Upnor Castle is shown, its guns firing, at the far right in the distance. To the left of the three burning ships near the centre of the picture the chain can just be made out and, protecting it from the bank, one of the 'two very slight batteries' that Evelyn observed*

of the raid, which he had witnessed 'from the Hill above Gillingham'. He apologized for having taken so long to send it, explaining he had been 'afflicted with the Griping of the Gutts'. He marked 'Upnore Castle', 'Chatham Yard', Rochester and Gillingham, among other places, and named and numbered in his key the warships on the Medway. The five he depicts (numbered 10, 11, 12, 13 and 14) in the loop of the river before Upnor and its small adjacent battery are the *Royal Charles*, which was captured by the Dutch, and the *Mary [Sancta Maria]*, *Royal Oak*, *Loyal London* and *Royal James* – all, he notes simply, 'Burnt'.

Above: *Sheerness Fort, with flag flying, in 1698, some 20 years after it was built by Sir Bernard de Gomme. To its right is Sheerness Dockyard; the mouth of the Medway lies to the left*
Below: *Upnor Castle in 1786. This engraving clearly shows, projecting through the palisade in front of the water bastion, the small jetty for powder boats. The storekeeper's house and barracks lie to the left of the castle*

the castle so as not to block their raiding vessels, followed the smaller sloops and fireships. Leading were de Ruyter and his senior commanders, rowed in longboats into the thick of the gunfire to encourage their men. Their fireships successfully set ablaze the *Loyal London*, the *Royal Oak* and the *Royal James*, but the unexpected intensity of the English fire from both sides of the river caused them to abandon further assaults. Next day they withdrew, taking the *Royal Charles* with them in triumph. For the English the disaster was only partly mitigated by Dutch failure to reach and destroy Chatham and any further shipping.

AFTER DEFEAT

After the raid the diarist John Evelyn visited Chatham and saw the burnt-out hulks, describing them as 'a Dreadful Spectacle as ever any English man saw and a dishonor never to be wiped off'. The humiliation galvanized the government into spending large sums of money over the next 15 years improving coastal fortifications, notably those protecting naval bases. Many of these defences were designed by Charles II's Chief Engineer, the Flemish Sir Bernard de Gomme. De Gomme's half-built Sheerness Fort at what is now Garrison Point on the Isle of Sheppey had been destroyed by the Dutch. So, immediately following the raid, in 1667, he designed a more powerful

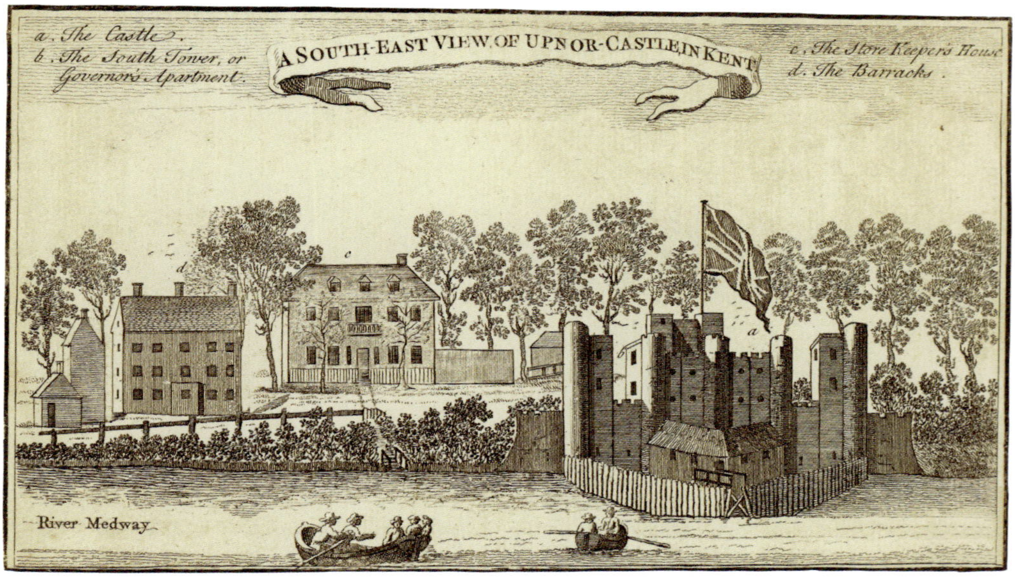

Left: *Two 32-pounder cannon beside the North Tower mounted on replica carriages. They were cast in 1859 by Walker & Co. of Rotherham for the Royal Navy and were among the last smooth-bore guns firing solid shot to be made*

Guns at the Castle

During its life as a fort the number of guns at Upnor varied greatly, depending on the state of war and funds.

Upnor was built when the main weapons for fortifications and warships were heavy guns firing solid iron or stone shot. The garrison also had muskets, but these were slow and cumbersome and well into the 17th century forts such as Upnor also kept stocks of longbows and arrows, which were comparatively light, quick to use, and lethal against attackers at close range.

A captain, normally a man of some standing in the county with millitary skills, would have been in charge of the garrison. Under him was the master gunner, an experienced artilleryman who commanded the gunners manning the fort's main armament. He was responsible for the guns and munitions and for training the gunners. The largest guns required teams of about six men to load, aim and fire them; smaller guns had proportionally fewer gunners. Not all the fort's guns would necessarily be in action at the same time, so gun crews could be responsible for more than one weapon. Where there were insufficient gunners, the garrison soldiers would help with less skilled activities, such as bringing up supplies of powder and shot.

The number of men and guns at Upnor varied greatly during its life as a fortress. Its first armament in 1567 is not known, but a 1603 survey lists the largest weapons here as a demi-cannon (firing 30lb shot), 7 culverins (long, thin cannons; 17lb shot), 5 demi-culverins (9lb shot) and a saker (small cannon; 5lb shot), together with a number of smaller guns.

Upnor's armament was probably at its peak at the start of the First Dutch War in 1652, when it had 15 demi-cannon, 19 culverins, 9 demi-culverins and 13 sakers; yet only one master gunner and eight gunners are listed on the inventory, suggesting not all the 45 guns were serviceable. Some earlier inventories mention 20 soldiers who would have been essential to help man the fort.

The guns were bronze or iron, the latter probably from the iron gun-founding industry in the Sussex Weald. Although these 17th-century guns could fire up to 1.5 miles, their effective ranges were only a few hundred yards. The majority would have been mounted on wooden truck carriages, covering the river and firing through the embrasures on the water bastion and main building. A few small weapons inside the towers would have been on timber beds firing on fixed bearings through gun loops.

***Above:** Upnor Castle in 1780. A hoy (a type of small coastal vessel widely used by the Board of Ordnance as a powder boat) lies alongside the water bastion jetty awaiting loading with powder barrels*

bastioned fort to replace it and to guard more effectively the mouth of the Medway and Sheerness Dockyard; traces of this fort survive among later defences. To protect warships at Chatham and Long Reach, de Gomme built two gun batteries, one at Cockham Wood, about a mile downriver from Upnor, and one at Gillingham, guarding the entrance to St Mary's Creek. Additional batteries were added at Hoo Ness and the Isle of Grain at the end of the 17th century.

UPNOR BECOMES A GUNPOWDER MAGAZINE

Even before the Dutch raid, the castle had begun to be used for the storage of gunpowder and munitions; it is known to have supplied warships anchored off Queenborough and the Nore in 1667. Although Upnor had acquitted itself creditably during the raid, de Gomme's new defences reduced its value as a fortress and in 1668 orders were given to convert it into 'a Place of Stores and Magazine' for the Board of Ordnance.

In its new role the castle was disarmed, although some of the garrison may have stayed to guard the site, probably lodging in the village with the main building now the powder magazine. The roof-level gun platforms were removed and the building was heightened slightly to make more storage space on the first floor. Its castellated appearance was retained. The North and South Towers were similarly treated. A single-storey shifting house (see page 15) was built on the water bastion and a jetty added to the bastion for powder boats to lie alongside. Just behind the castle the storekeeper was provided with a new residence, now part of Castle House (in private ownership).

A 1691 survey of ordnance and stores at Upnor reveals its new importance: as well as 5,206 barrels of powder, there were 164 iron guns, 62 standing carriages, 100 ships' carriages, 7,125 round shot, more than 200 muskets and 77 pikes. A century later, as the Navy grew in size, increasing numbers of warships (sometimes captured enemy prizes, or old, decommissioned Royal Navy ships) had to be moored nearby as floating, supplementary magazines.

LABORATORY, PROOF YARD AND MUSEUM

By 1806 the South Tower was a laboratory (see page 10) and the North Tower housed munitions and lumber. The gatehouse was apparently derelict. From 1808 new magazines and other facilities began to be added outside the castle, joined at the end of the 19th century by vast magazines at Chattenden and Lodge Hill. Upnor's use gradually declined: hoisting powder barrels into its main building was laborious and potentially dangerous, and the comparatively narrow passage through the gatehouse inconvenient. Although the Napoleonic Wars (1803–15) kept the magazine in use, by 1812 it held only 3,500 barrels. In 1827 its use as a major store was largely discontinued, except in emergencies, as in the Crimean War (1853–6), when 16,500 shells had to be stored from the fleet returning from the Baltic.

From the 1830s, the castle was mainly an ordnance laboratory with the courtyard a proof yard for testing firearms and gunpowder. Limited powder and, later, guncotton (chemically treated cotton, used as an explosive) were kept in the main building into the mid 1890s. From here they were taken to the water bastion where, by the 1850s, the former shifting house had been turned into a laboratory.

Laboratory workers repaired ammunition and, from the 1860s, as cylindrical shells for the new rifled guns began to replace the old solid shot of the smooth-bore guns, they became responsible for filling and emptying shells and cartridges with explosives, and servicing their fuses. This work was probably moved to new shell-filling rooms completed north of the castle in 1907. In 1891 the castle and its ordnance facilities were transferred from the War Office (which had subsumed the Board of Ordnance) to the Admiralty. The naval arms race with Germany saw an unprecedented expansion of the Royal

Above: *A wounded veteran of the Crimean War at Chatham. After the war, the returning fleet brought back troops and munitions, including unused shells, 16,500 of these were stored at Upnor Castle*

Below: *Upnor Castle in about 1856 by Henry Pether. In the distance on the opposite side of the river stands the newly completed range of covered building slips in Chatham Dockyard*

Right: *The ordnance yard beside Upnor Castle photographed in the 1940s. In the centre are two lines of shell-filling rooms of 1905–8 and to the left the 19th-century powder magazines. The castle can be seen through the trees*

Below: *Upnor Castle from the south-west; the gun-ports in the gatehouse and South Tower were carefully positioned to provide covering fire along the faces of the curtain wall*

Navy and by 1900 the creation of the huge naval ordnance establishments near Upnor at Lodge Hill and Chattenden. The castle consequently lost importance, but with munition storage space at a premium here during the First World War use of it and its proof yard continued into the early 1920s.

By then, the castle's historic importance was appreciated and it found a new use as an unofficial site museum, with a growing collection of artefacts, from Roman pottery to cannon balls, collected from the area by ordnance staff and others. During the Second World War the castle suffered slight damage from air raids in 1941. In 1945, after the war, the Admiralty gave official approval for the castle to be used as a museum; over the next few years war damage was repaired and some restoration undertaken. In 1961 responsibility for the care of Upnor Castle and its barracks was assumed by the State and in 1984 passed to English Heritage, where it remains today. Both castle and barracks are managed by Medway Council.